CLOZE Practice Book

For CEM style 11+ test preparation

Gulliford Tutors

Contents

	Page
Foreword	3
Three Missing Letters	4
Fill in the Missing Letters	30
Word Banks	60

Foreword

CLOZE tests are an important part of the 11+ CEM tests. These are tasks where you have to fill in the blanks in a passage of text. Possibly the hardest questions asked are those where you not only must know the word but also how to spell it!

There are three types of CLOZE tests included in this book:

- **Missing three letter words** - One word in each sentence has three missing letters which happen to make up a three letter word *e.g. The afternoon on the lake was relaxing and **PEA**ceful.* You must use the sentence to help you work out the word needed to complete the sentence so that it makes sense.

- **Fill in the missing letters** - some of the words in a text have missing letters. You must use the text to recognise what the missing word is and then use your spelling knowledge to fill in the missing letters.

- **Word Bank** - some of the words in a text have been taken out and placed in a list called a 'word bank'. You must fill in the blanks in the text by choosing the most appropriate word from the word bank.

Using a strategy to complete these tests is crucial:

- Learn as many word meanings as possible. Keep a notebook and list words you don't know, find out their meaning and learn them.

- Go through the test filling in any words you know straight away.

- Go back and look at prefixes which fit e.g. pre-, re-, con-, -ing, -ed, -ght.

- Now check again as you may suddenly have an inspired moment of memory!

- With the word bank, only put in words you are certain are correct on your first run-through. Tick off words you use in the word bank so you can easily see which ones are left. On your second run-through the text, it should be easier to figure out which word goes where as you have fewer words to choose from.

Test 1

In each question, a three letter word has been removed from one of the words. Complete each word so that the sentence makes sense.

1. She was very apo____etic when she broke the window

2. The tree branch was b____ing dangerously in the wind

3. The mask he wore was g____esque and frightening

4. They defi____ly ignored their mother's orders

5. The girls had ar____ged to meet outside the cinema

6. The train was de____ting from platform 2

7. She had as____ed that they knew what to do

8. We shall def____ our country, whatever the cost

9. The match will go on, wh____ver the weather

10. The w____her is glorious in Spain today

Test 2

In each question, a three letter word has been removed from one of the words. Complete each word so that the sentence makes sense.

1. The snow was w____e and sparkling

2. The roads were closed because it was s____ing heavily

3. The king was ____rayed by his treacherous brother

4. Keeping wild animals in ____tivity is cruel

5. She saw the speeding lorry in her perip____al vision

6. My friend is rather p____ial to bacon sandwiches

7. Her trousers and shirt were in coor____ating colours

8. The bully was a weak, co____dly man

9. The football team suffered a devastating def____

10. He had been physically de____med by a rare bone disease

Test 3

In each question, a three letter word has been removed from one of the words. Complete each word so that the sentence makes sense.

1. The young boy had acci____tally broken the precious vase

2. On the sunny day, their teacher had ex____ded breaktime

3. The foam ex____ded when water was added

4. The owner of the lost dog was unk____n

5. The rescued cat was very ti____ and shy

6. Our walk to the top of the mountain was ar____us

7. He had been edu____ed to university level

8. All referees must remain im____tial

9. He was wearing a bright, flam____ant bow tie

10. Her flip____t remark upset her best friend

Test 4

In each question, a three letter word has been removed from one of the words.
Complete each word so that the sentence makes sense.

1. They loved to travel around ___eign countries

2. The child would not share her toys because she was s___ish

3. The goalie de___ded all the attacks on his goal

4. It is il___al to park on double yellow lines

5. Helen continued reading her book, igno___t of the danger

6. The puppy was reluc___t to let go of her favourite toy

7. The stray dog looked at him with sor___ful eyes

8. Many chemicals can be h___ful to your skin

9. I don't walk in the mountains without consul___g my map

10. The boy exhibited a thirst for kn___edge

Test 5

In each question, a three letter word has been removed from one of the words. Complete each word so that the sentence makes sense.

1. It was im___bable that the match would proceed in the snow

2. They were ___ried in the village church

3. Their teacher was angry at their juve___e behaviour

4. She behaved in a ___ure and polite manner

5. He always wrote the mini___ amount allowed

6. The cost of restoring the church has been im___se

7. Their work was careless and s___dash

8. The newspaper article contains many mis___ding statements

9. Sandy deserts are dry and a___ – a harsh environment to live

10. My sister's bedroom is meticulou___ clean compared to mine

Test 6

In each question, a three letter word has been removed from one of the words. Complete each word so that the sentence makes sense.

1. The va____t sign on the toilet told me it was empty

2. The dog was over____ed when her owner returned home

3. The young child was f____ful of spiders

4. The police car was fol____ing the suspicious vehicle closely

5. The design was beautifully complex and elabo____e

6. The children bumped into each other accident____y

7. Lines which meet at right angles are per____dicular

8. The audience broke into spon____eous applause

9. The attack was premedit____d and vicious

10. He had had a pro____able day selling his goods at the market

Test 7

In each question, a three letter word has been removed from one of the words. Complete each word so that the sentence makes sense.

1. They were s____ing at the lunar eclipse in amazement

2. Make sure you are ____ctual in the morning

3. The storm ____ed throughout the night, keeping everyone awake

4. Peter's best fri____ always walked to school with him

5. The sc____ity of food on the island was very worrying

6. The teacher held her hands to____her as if she was praying

7. The ____iance between the countries helped to win the war

8. The countries were u____ed in their belief that peace was essential

9. The daylight hours shor____ in the winter

10. Mum fr____ed at us when we giggled in church

Test 8

In each question, a three letter word has been removed from one of the words. Complete each word so that the sentence makes sense.

1. He was charged with driving a vehicle while intoxi____ed

2. Mum volunteered to wash the football team's s____ed kit

3. Grandad is always a good lis____er if you have worries

4. The horse was munching hay in his warm s____le

5. My ____cher was pleased with my excellent test score

6. The idea of aliens is the____tical as it hasn't been proved

7. The snake was ____ocuous and harmless

8. He was a simple and unsop____ticated young man

9. I ate the ent____ cake but then felt sick

10. The child's behaviour was volatile and unpredic____le

Test 9

In each question, a three letter word has been removed from one of the words. Complete each word so that the sentence makes sense.

1. Urban areas have a high population and are very built up
2. The giant was the v___ain of the story
3. The group of volun___rs worked tirelessly all day
4. Compri___g of 50 states, the USA is a very large country
5. They had to be quiet so they were whis___ing
6. They waited im___iently for the doors of the shop to open
7. I don't like the ___ter as it is cold
8. Glass contr___s as it cools
9. When the mouse saw the cat, it went ___id with terror
10. I haven't been totally h___st with you

Test 10

In each question, a three letter word has been removed from one of the words.
Complete each word so that the sentence makes sense.

1. At the end of the marathon he was overcome with ___igue

2. Ti___ness overcame her and she fell into a deep sleep

3. Slumped in the chair, there was an air of ___hargy about him

4. As he neared the end of his journey, he felt immense w___iness

5. She gave a f___less performance to win the prize

6. The signature on the cheque was ___ged

7. The cocker spaniel dog was ___ite and beautiful

8. The stain on the carpet was small and insignifi___t

9. The council imposed huge fines for tri___l parking offences

10. The young man earned a pal___ £2 a day for his paper round

Test 11

In each question, a three letter word has been removed from one of the words. Complete each word so that the sentence makes sense.

1. She felt that the colour of her dress was ___mportant

2. The footballers were ___dy as they celebrated their victory

3. The ener___ic toddler ran around the garden for hours

4. They watched an ani___ed film version of the fairy-tale

5. The team are ___eful of a win today

6. I was nervous but my friend gave me an encou___ing smile

7. There's no point in desp___ing when things get tough

8. She was very appre___sive before her driving test

9. His ___oic actions saved the girl's life

10. The horse was f___ful of going into the water

Test 12

In each question, a three letter word has been removed from one of the words.
Complete each word so that the sentence makes sense.

1. The dish____st man stole a book from the shop

2. The woman was po____ive that she had left her purse on the bus

3. The a____dance of birthday presents made her very happy

4. When the Queen is in resi____ce, the Union Jack flies high

5. The grey storm clouds obscu____ the sun

6. The woman was f____tic when she thought she had lost her dog

7. The talented runner was ____sistently placed first

8. The in____ent child ignored the man's instructions

9. The vicar was boring as he kept ____bling on

10. It was pleasant to ____der through the beautiful gardens

Test 13

In each question, a three letter word has been removed from one of the words. Complete each word so that the sentence makes sense.

1. That area of common-land was char ___ by the bushfire

2. The king hoped that his army would ___ quish their enemy

3. The defe ___ d champions were extremely disappointed

4. She conqu ___ d her fear of dogs by walking her friend's pet

5. Our mum was extremely i ___ e when we broke the window

6. The students were en ___ ed at the ban on mobile phones

7. The rider cajo ___ the nervous horse into the horsebox

8. The hungry man was tempted to s ___ l food from the market stall

9. It was easy to ___ ate the image on the computer

10. The famous adventurer climbed his final mountain ___ k

Test 14

In each question, a three letter word has been removed from one of the words.
Complete each word so that the sentence makes sense.

1. She scrambled up the path to the ____mit

2. Her exhi____ at the flower show won the top prize

3. The power cut lead to the sus____sion of the play

4. The apple was missh____n and looked like a face

5. It had been a very p____uctive day

6. Once the repair man had been, the TV was wor____g again

7. If I let the dog off the lead, she will run away and di____pear

8. Achilles' bravery was ____endary

9. Thor is a god mentioned in many a Viking ____a

10. The footballer received a repri____d for a dangerous tackle

Test 15

In each question, a three letter word has been removed from one of the words. Complete each word so that the sentence makes sense.

1. The prince was the legiti____e heir to the throne

2. The letter from Churchill is regarded as an aut____tic document

3. The beg____ing of the film was terribly exciting

4. Scrooge's ____mer partner was called Jacob Marley

5. You should be as____ed of your behaviour

6. Use of mobiles in school is a very con____tious issue

7. The lady was too fru____ to splash out on designer clothes

8. The fr____ old lady needed to be rushed to the hospital

9. It was unf____ that I was punished but my sister wasn't

10. The TV report might prejud____ the jury's decision

Test 16

In each question, a three letter word has been removed from one of the words.
Complete each word so that the sentence makes sense.

1. I shall de____itely be at the train station to collect you
2. I stayed up until I had watched the comp____e film
3. Her behaviour was inelegant and un____ined
4. The old woman was hood____ked into giving money
5. The dangerous building had to be demoli____d
6. He continued to repair the old rusty contr____ion
7. The aggressive player delib____tely hit her with a hockey stick
8. My parents store h____ful chemicals in a locked cupboard
9. The weather is unfav____able for sailing today
10. The old buil____g had ornate columns and beautiful statues

Test 17

In each question, a three letter word has been removed from one of the words.
Complete each word so that the sentence makes sense.

1. He was pes____istic about the future

2. The cottage was pe____ful while the family were out

3. He was ch____ed after he had walked in the rain for two hours

4. The paralympics include wheelch____ races

5. The man cast a s____ow on the pavement

6. The com____ed age of the three sisters was one hundred

7. He paddled in the shal____ water

8. The athlete ran the race at a s____dy pace

9. The ruler s____ped when the child bent it too far

10. They ar____ged to meet in town on Saturday afternoon

Test 18

In each question, a three letter word has been removed from one of the words. Complete each word so that the sentence makes sense.

1. The boys hated s____ping with their mum
2. The children loved ____dling in the sea
3. The girl decided to ret____ the jumper because it was too big
4. The brave boy received a re____d for finding the stolen goods
5. Prepo____ions descibe the location of a noun
6. Flamenco is a traditional s____ish dance
7. I've had an ar____ent with my brother
8. She competed in a____eur athletics competitions
9. My mother is often very em____rassing
10. A rectangle has two lines of sym____ry

Test 19

In each question, a three letter word has been removed from one of the words. Complete each word so that the sentence makes sense.

1. She has an extensive knowledge of vo____ulary

2. She sum____ised the story accurately and succinctly

3. My dad hit his t____bnail accidentally with the hammer

4. The opposite of active is p____ive

5. The days leng____n in the summer

6. He had so much energy that he appeared inde____igable

7. The study of nature is called bio____y

8. The miserly old man h____ded his money

9. I was he____ant to jump off the diving board

10. He was too b____ful to come out and meet the stranger

Test 20

In each question, a three letter word has been removed from one of the words. Complete each word so that the sentence makes sense.

1. He had spent too much money and was in fi____cial difficulties
2. Cold weather inhi____s plant growth
3. It is easy to mi____terpret a situation
4. An eight sided polygon is called an oc____on
5. You must be pa____nt and wait your turn
6. The old dog tol____ntly allowed the puppy play with its tail
7. His membership had run out and was now inva____
8. The donkey is one of the most obs____ate animals on Earth
9. The diplomat's reply was very t____ful
10. The rangers worked t____lessly to rescue the trapped elk

Test 21

In each question, a three letter word has been removed from one of the words. Complete each word so that the sentence makes sense.

1. We must protect our planet as our resources are not in____ite

2. The rowdy audience int____upted the actor's speech

3. There is always so____hing to see and do at the seaside

4. The accu____ion against the boy was false

5. He was a ____hteous person who stood up for the truth

6. It was a real surprise when his vi____ors turned up early

7. The mi____es seemed to pass slowly during that boring lesson

8. It has become increa____gly difficult to find my favourite sweets

9. It was not yet 9 o' clock, so pre____ably the boys were still awake

10. The children were told off for running in the cor____or

Test 22

In each question, a three letter word has been removed from one of the words.
Complete each word so that the sentence makes sense.

1. She did not perform well because she hadn't taken it seriou____

2. The farmer walked di____nally across the field

3. She brought her com____ion along to the party

4. They all went to____her in the same car

5. She was very excited when she set off on her ho____ay to Spain

6. It was a sunny day so breakfast was served on the terr____

7. It was the ele____t of danger which gave him his love of flying

8. She felt extremely na____ous during the bumpy car journey

9. The afternoon on the lake was relaxing and ____ceful

10. Julia is very good at re____nising wild flowers

Three Missing Letters Answers

Test 1
1. log
2. end
3. rot
4. ant
5. ran
6. par
7. sum
8. end
9. ate
10. eat

Test 2
1. hit
2. now
3. bet
4. cap
5. her
6. art
7. din
8. war
9. eat
10. for

Test 3
1. den
2. ten
3. pan
4. now
5. mid
6. duo
7. cat
8. par
9. boy
10. pan

Test 4
1. for
2. elf
3. fen
4. leg
5. ran
6. tan
7. row
8. arm
9. tin
10. owl

Test 5
1. pro
2. mar
3. nil
4. mat
5. mum
6. men
7. lap
8. lea
9. rid
10. sly

Test 6
1. can
2. joy
3. ear
4. low
5. rat
6. all
7. pen
8. tan
9. ate
10. fit

Test 7
1. tar
2. pun
3. rag
4. end
5. arc
6. get
7. all
8. nit
9. ten
10. own

Test 8
1. cat
2. oil
3. ten
4. tab
5. tea
6. ore
7. inn
8. his
9. ire
10. tab

Test 9
1. ban
2. ill
3. tee
4. sin
5. per
6. pat
7. win
8. act
9. rig
10. one

Test 10
1. fat
2. red
3. let
4. ear
5. law
6. for
7. pet
8. can
9. via
10. try

Test 11
1. uni
2. row
3. get
4. mat
5. hop
6. rag
7. air
8. hen
9. her
10. ear

Test 12
1. one
2. sit
3. bun
4. den
5. red
6. ran
7. con
8. sol
9. ram
10. wan

Test 13
1. red
2. van
3. ate
4. ere
5. rat
6. rag
7. led
8. tea
9. rot
10. pea

Test 14
1. sum
2. bit
3. pen
4. ape
5. rod
6. kin
7. sap
8. leg
9. sag
10. man

Test 15
1. mat
2. hen
3. inn
4. for
5. ham
6. ten
7. gal
8. ail
9. air
10. ice

Test 16
1. fin
2. let
3. ref
4. win
5. she
6. apt
7. era
8. arm
9. our
10. din

Test 17
1. sim
2. ace
3. ill
4. air
5. had
6. bin
7. low
8. tea
9. nap
10. ran

Test 18
1. hop
2. pad
3. urn
4. war
5. sit
6. pan
7. gum
8. mat
9. bar
10. met

Test 19

1. cab
2. mar
3. hum
4. ass
5. the
6. fat
7. log
8. oar
9. sit
10. ash

Test 20

1. nan
2. bit
3. sin
4. tag
5. tie
6. era
7. lid
8. tin
9. act
10. ire

Test 21

1. fin
2. err
3. met
4. sat
5. rig
6. sit
7. nut
8. sin
9. sum
10. rid

Test 22

1. sly
2. ago
3. pan
4. get
5. lid
6. ace
7. men
8. use
9. pea
10. cog

Passage 1: Devon

Letters have been removed from some of the words in this passage. Complete these words so that the passage makes sense.

Devon is a county in southwest England. It is bordered by Cornwall, Somerset and Dorset. It encompasses sandy beaches, fossil cliffs, medieval towns and moorland national parks. Both Dartmoor with its granite tors and wild ponies and Exmoor comprise rugged (1) l☐☐☐ds☐ap☐s, purple heather moorland and green valleys. The (2) op☐☐☐tuni☐☐es for walkers are immense: the moors encourage younger walkers to get out and about, (3) e☐pe☐i☐☐ly during the annual Ten Tors Weekend. In (4) ☐dd☐ti☐n, the South West Coast Path follows the Devon coastline, taking in the towering cliffs of the northern Exmoor Coast and rock (5) ☐or☐☐ti☐ns on the fossil-rich southern Jurassic Coast from Exmouth. Lyme Regis is world reknowned for its fossil deposits. Various fossils of large (6) ☐in☐s☐urs have been found, some displayed at its dinosaur museum.

Devonshire cream teas are a treat for (7) t☐☐ri☐ts. In Devon, the cream is placed on the scone before the jam. In Cornwall, the jam goes on first. A great place to visit is the city of Exeter which was (8) ☐r☐g☐n☐lly built by the Romans who called it Isca. The cathedral dates back to medieval times.

Devon is a county with stunning landscapes, (9) ☐ran☐u☐l river valleys, long coastlines with opportunities to partake in (10) w☐te☐☐port☐ such as sailing, paddleboarding, canoeing, fishing and far more.

Passage 2: Dolphins

Letters have been removed from some of the words in this passage. Complete these words so that the passage makes sense.

Dolphins are aquatic (1) m☐m☐☐ls with species which live in the (2) o☐☐☐ns and some which live in rivers. There are forty (3) ☐pe☐ie☐ named as Dolphins. The males are usually larger than the females. Although dolphins are found all over the (4) w☐rl☐, most species prefer warmer waters in the tropics but there are species such as the Right Whale dolphin which prefer colder (5) cl☐☐at☐s.

The killer whale is actually a species of dolphin which can grow to 9.5 metres (6) l☐n☐ and weigh 10 tons. These, unlike most dolphins, feed on small mammals like seals. However other species of dolphin feed primarily on (7) f☐☐h and squid.

The (8) ☐o☐ng of the dolphin are called calves. These are usually born in spring or (9) ☐☐mme☐ when the waters are warmer and weather is less stormy. The mothers look after and raise their young and will nurse them for quite a long (10) p☐r☐☐d of time.

They have very (11) str☐☐mlin☐☐ bodies which allow them to swim at (12) s☐☐eds up to 35 miles per hour. Their conical shaped teeth help them to catch fish swimming at speed past them. Some species have adapted to their (13) ☐☐vir☐n☐ents such as those which dive to great depths and others which have a larger (14) l☐☐er of fat under their skin to (15) ☐☐sulate them in very cold water. They all have well- developed hearing and it is thought that they can survive even if blind because their hearing is so good.

Dolphins are highly intelligent and like to amuse themselves around boats and humans. However, humans are threatening their (16) s☐r☐iva☐ through habitat loss and sea pollution. Large fishing nets are also a threat to them as they are often caught up in the nets.

Passage 3: Florence Nightingale

Letters have been removed from some of the words in this passage. Complete these words so that the passage makes sense.

Florence Nightingale was born in Florence, Italy in 1820. She came from a (1) w☐☐lth☐ family and unlike many women at that time, she was educated. By the age of seventeen, she knew that she wanted to be a nurse. Nursing was not seen as a (2) c☐re☐☐ for educated women, so her father was not keen for her to do this. However in 1851 she (3) t☐a☐e☐☐ed to Germany to train, returning to London and running a hospital.

The Crimean War (4) b☐o☐e out in 1853 and Florence (5) vol☐☐te☐☐ed to go and help. On seeing the military hospitals, she was (6) ☐☐pal☐ed by the lack of hygiene and the awful (7) c☐n☐it☐☐ns there. She worked tirelessly to (8) t☐☐ns☐or☐ the wards into clean, light and (9) effi☐☐en☐ places. She made sure that all patients were washed, dressings changed and patients were fed properly.

The patient death-rate decreased (10) d☐☐ama☐ic☐ll☐. The wounded soldiers called her 'The lady of the lamp' because she would wander through the wards at night, checking that her patients were (11) c☐m☐☐rt☐☐le.

When she returned to England, she was already famous and a national (12) h☐☐oi☐e. She raised money to start a college for nurses and trained them in the (13) i☐☐ort☐nc☐ of hygiene and proper diet for a good (14) ☐e☐o☐ery. In 1907, she received the Order of Merit which is given to citizens who make an important (15) c☐☐tr☐but☐on to society. She was the first woman to receive this. Quite rightly so as she changed nursing into a skilled and well-respected profession.

Passage 4: An Extract from Jemima Puddle-duck

Letters have been removed from some of the words in this passage. Complete these words so that the passage makes sense.

Jemima Puddle-duck was not much in the habit of flying. She ran downhill a few yards (1) ☐la☐pi☐g her wings, and then she jumped off into the air. She flew (2) b☐☐☐tiful☐y when she had got a good start. She skimmed along over the (3) ☐re☐t☐ps until she saw an open place in the middle of the wood, where the trees and brushwood had been cleared. Jemima alighted rather heavily and began to (4) ☐ad☐☐e about in search of a (5) co☐v☐n☐☐nt dry nesting place. She rather fancied a tree (6) s☐u☐☐ amongst some tall foxgloves. But—seated upon the stump, she was startled to find an (7) el☐☐antl☐ dressed gentleman reading a (8) ne☐☐pa☐er. He had black prick ears and sandy colored whiskers. (9) "☐ua☐k?" said Jemima Puddle-duck, with her head and her bonnet on the one side— "Quack?"

The gentleman raised his eyes above his newspaper and looked curiously at Jemima— "Madam, have you lost your way?" said he. He had a long bushy tail which he was (10) si☐☐☐ng upon, as the stump was somewhat damp.

Passage 5: An Extract from 'Oliver Twist'

Letters have been removed from some of the words in this passage. Complete these words so that the passage makes sense.

The room in which the boys were fed, was a large stone hall, with a copper at one end: out of which the master, (1) ☐re☐se☐ in an apron for the purpose, and (2) a☐s☐st☐d by one or two women, ladled the gruel at mealtimes. Of this festive composition each boy had one porringer, and no more - (3) e☐☐ep☐ on occasions of great public rejoicing, when he had two ounces and a quarter of (4) br☐☐d besides.

The bowls never wanted washing. The boys (5) p☐☐is☐ed them with their spoons till they shone again; and when they had performed this (6) o☐er☐t☐on (which never took very long, the spoons being nearly as large as the bowls), they would sit staring at the copper, with such eager eyes, as if they could have (7) ☐e☐our☐d the very bricks of which it was composed; employing themselves, meanwhile, in (8) s☐c☐ing their fingers most assiduously, with the view of catching up any stray splashes of gruel that might have been cast thereon. Boys have generally excellent appetites. Oliver Twist and his (9) co☐pa☐io☐s suffered the tortures of slow (10) s☐a☐va☐ion for three months: at last they got so voracious and wild with (11) h☐ng☐r, that one boy, who was tall for his age, and hadn't been used to that sort of thing (for his father had kept a small cook-shop), hinted darkly to his companions, that unless he had another basin of gruel per diem, he was (12) a☐r☐☐d he might some night happen to eat the boy who slept next him, who happened to be a weakly youth of tender age. He had a wild, hungry eye; and they implicitly (13) bel☐☐☐ed him. A (14) c☐☐nci☐ was held; lots were cast who should walk up to the master after supper that evening, and ask for more; and it fell to Oliver Twist.

The evening arrived; the boys took their places. The master, in his cook's (15) ☐n☐for☐, stationed himself at the copper; his pauper assistants ranged themselves behind him; the gruel was served out; and a long grace was said over the short commons. The gruel disappeared; the boys (16) w☐is☐e☐ed to each other, and (17) ☐ink☐d at Oliver; while his next neighbours nudged him. Child as he was, he was (18) de☐☐era☐e with hunger, and reckless with misery. He rose from the table; and (19) ☐dv☐n☐ing to the master, basin and spoon in hand, said: somewhat alarmed at his own temerity:

'Please, sir, I want some (20) m☐r☐.'

Passage 6: An Extract from 'Peter Pan'

Letters have been removed from some of the words in this passage. Complete these words so that the passage makes sense.

Mrs Darling first heard of Peter when she was tidying up her children's minds. It is the (1) n☐☐htl☐ custom of every good mother after her children are asleep to (2) ☐um☐☐ge in their minds and put things straight for next morning, repacking into their proper places the many (3) ☐r☐ic☐es that have wandered during the day. If you could keep awake (but of course you can't) you would see your own mother doing this, and you would find it very interesting to watch her. It is quite like (4) ☐idy☐ng up drawers. You would see her on her knees, I expect, lingering (5) ☐umou☐ou☐ly over some of your contents, wondering where on earth you had picked this thing up, making (6) di☐☐ov☐r☐es sweet and not so sweet, pressing this to her cheek as if it were as nice as a kitten, and hurriedly stowing that out of sight. When you wake in the morning, the naughtinesses and evil passions with which you went to bed have been folded up small and placed at the bottom of your mind, and on the top, beautifully aired, are spread out your prettier thoughts, ready for you to put on.

Occasionally in her travels through her children's minds Mrs Darling found things she could not (7) u☐d☐r☐☐ and, and of these quite the most (8) ☐☐rpl☐xin☐ was the word Peter. She knew of no Peter, and yet he was here and there in John and Michael's minds, while Wendy's began to be scrawled all over with him. The name stood out in bolder letters than any of the other words, and as Mrs Darling gazed she felt that it had an oddly cocky (9) a☐pe☐☐an☐e. "Yes, he is rather cocky," Wendy (10) a☐m☐t☐☐d with regret. Her mother had been questioning her. "But who is he, my pet?" "He is Peter Pan, you know, Mother."

At first Mrs Darling did not know, but after thinking back into her (11) c☐☐☐dh☐☐d she just remembered a Peter Pan who was said to live with the fairies. There were many peculiar (12) sto☐☐e☐ about him. She had believed in him at the time, but now that she was married and full of sense she quite doubted whether there was any such person.

Passage 7: Queen Elizabeth II

Letters have been removed from some of the words in this passage. Complete these words so that the passage makes sense.

Queen Elizabeth II is now the longest (1) re☐☐ni☐g British monarch in history having now surpassed Queen Victoria , her great-great (2) gr☐n☐mo☐☐er, who was the reigned for 63 years. Queen Elizabeth is (3) ☐ona☐rc☐ of 16 of the 53 Commonwealth countries. She (4) c☐☐☐bra☐ed her Diamond jubilee, 60 years of rule, in 2012.

She was born as Princess Elizabeth on April 23rd 1926 in London. Her parents were Prince Albert, Duke of York and Elizabeth Bowes-Lyon. Her father was not expected to be (5) k☐☐g but after the abdication of his brother, Edward VIII so that he could marry the divorcee Wallis Simpson, Prince Albert became King George VI.

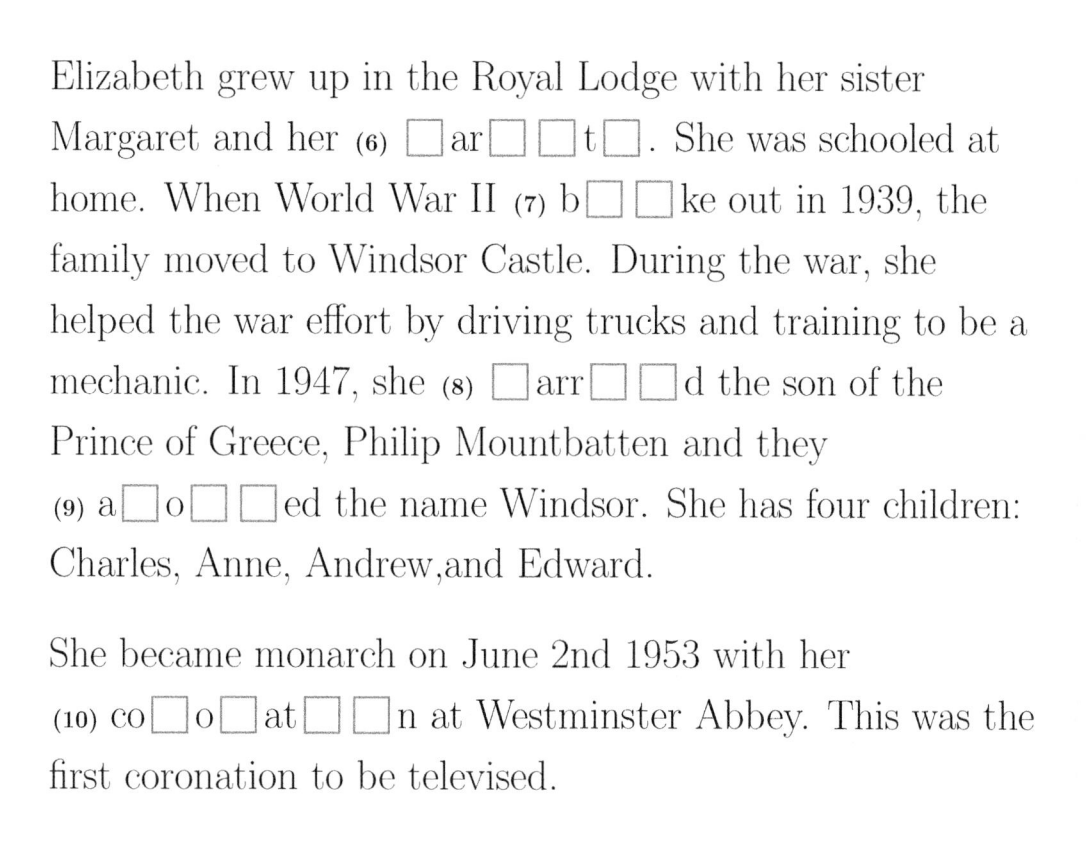

Elizabeth grew up in the Royal Lodge with her sister Margaret and her (6) ☐ar☐ ☐t☐. She was schooled at home. When World War II (7) b☐ ☐ke out in 1939, the family moved to Windsor Castle. During the war, she helped the war effort by driving trucks and training to be a mechanic. In 1947, she (8) ☐arr☐ ☐d the son of the Prince of Greece, Philip Mountbatten and they (9) a☐o☐ ☐ed the name Windsor. She has four children: Charles, Anne, Andrew,and Edward.

She became monarch on June 2nd 1953 with her (10) co☐o☐at☐ ☐n at Westminster Abbey. This was the first coronation to be televised.

Passage 8: Snowdonia National Park

Letters have been removed from some of the words in this passage. Complete these words so that the passage makes sense.

Snowdonia is a region in northwest Wales concentrated around the (1) m☐☐nt☐☐ns and glacial landforms of Snowdonia National Park. The park was (2) e☐☐a☐lis☐ed in 1951 as Britain's third national park. As well as being the largest National Park in Wales, Snowdonia (3) b☐a☐☐s the highest mountain in England and Wales, and the (4) l☐r☐e☐t natural lake in Wales, as well as a wealth of (5) p☐ct☐☐es☐ue villages like Betws y Coed and Beddgelert.

Snowdonia is an area steeped in (6) ☐u☐t☐☐e and local history, where more than half its (7) p☐☐u☐a☐ion speak Welsh. Since 1896, visitors have used the park's historic Snowdon Mountain Railway to climb to the (8) s☐m☐☐t of Mount Snowdon, offering views across the sea to Ireland. The park is also home to over 100 lakes and craggy peaks like Cader Idris and Tryfan.

Snowdonia is one of the wettest parts of the United Kingdom; Crib Goch in Snowdonia is the wettest spot in the United Kingdom, with an (9) a☐☐ra☐e rainfall of 4,473 millimetres a year .

Legend has it that Snowdon is the burial place of the giant ogre Rhita, (10) ☐anq☐i☐hed by King Arthur. It is believed that Arthur's Knights still sleep beneath.

Passage 9: How the geese saved Rome

Letters have been removed from some of the words in this passage. Complete these words so that the passage makes sense.

At the height of Rome's power, the Roman (1) E☐p☐☐e spread throughout Europe and beyond as the Roman armies (2) co☐q☐er☐d nation after nation. However, 2,400 years ago, the Gauls were (3) in☐a☐i☐☐ Italy and had attacked the city of Rome. After they had (4) ☐a☐ch☐d up from the Tiber, they had conquered all of the city (5) e☐☐ept for the Capitoline Hill which the Roman army was defending vigorously.

(6) L☐☐☐nd has it that on a clear and starry night with a full moon, the bravest of the Gallic soldiers (7) ☐t☐althi☐y climbed up the steep sides of this high outcrop and were so quiet that they didn't wake either the Roman soldiers who were supposedly (8) g☐☐r☐i☐g the hill or the guard dogs in their kennels.

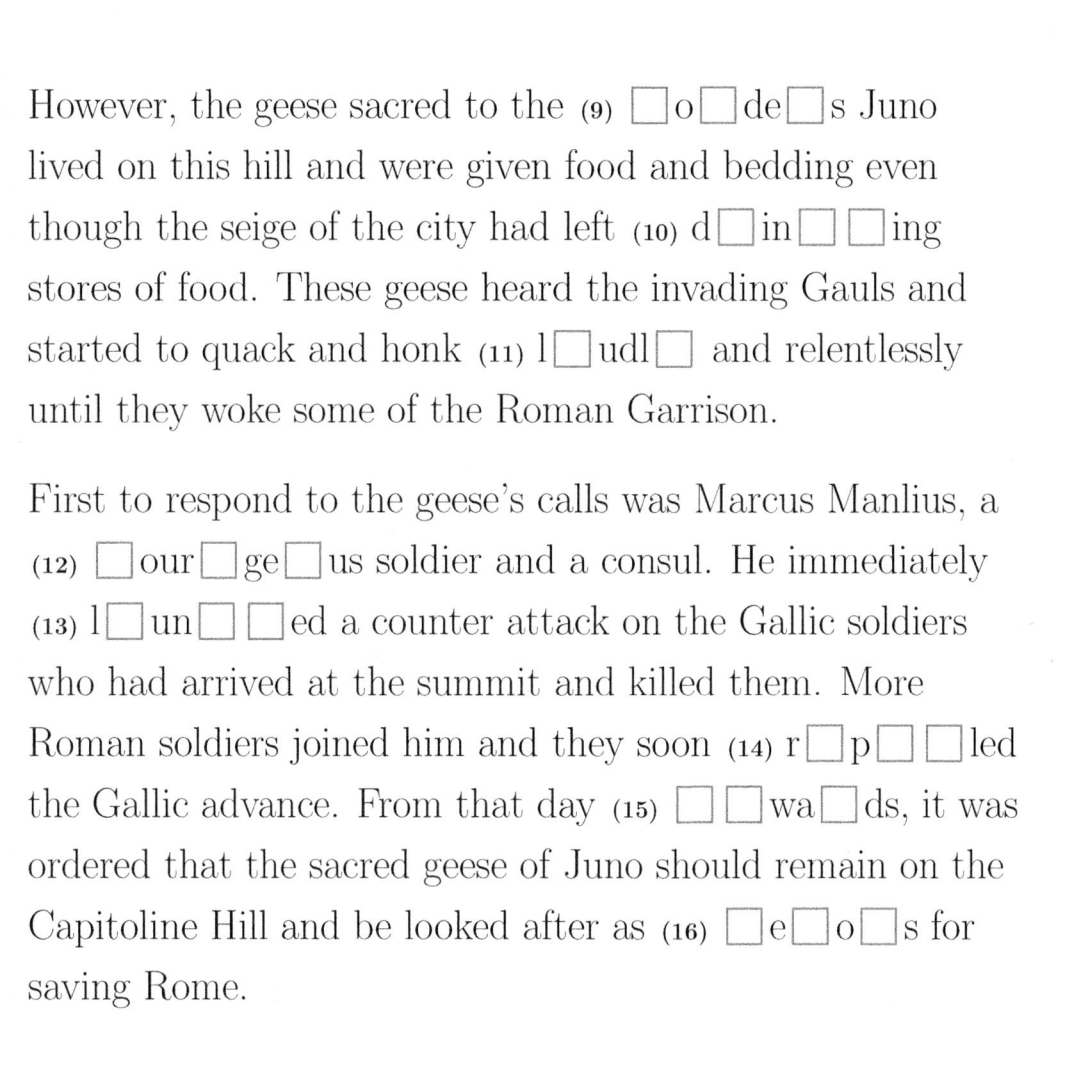

However, the geese sacred to the (9) ☐o☐de☐s Juno lived on this hill and were given food and bedding even though the seige of the city had left (10) d☐in☐☐ing stores of food. These geese heard the invading Gauls and started to quack and honk (11) l☐udl☐ and relentlessly until they woke some of the Roman Garrison.

First to respond to the geese's calls was Marcus Manlius, a (12) ☐our☐ge☐us soldier and a consul. He immediately (13) l☐un☐☐ed a counter attack on the Gallic soldiers who had arrived at the summit and killed them. More Roman soldiers joined him and they soon (14) r☐p☐☐led the Gallic advance. From that day (15) ☐☐wa☐ds, it was ordered that the sacred geese of Juno should remain on the Capitoline Hill and be looked after as (16) ☐e☐o☐s for saving Rome.

Passage 10: An extract from 'Treasure Island'

Letters have been removed from some of the words in this passage. Complete these words so that the passage makes sense.

I remember him as if it were (1) ☐es☐er☐a☐, as he came (2) pl☐ddin☐ to the inn door, his sea-chest following (3) ☐eh☐☐d him in a hand-barrow. He was tall, strong, heavy, nut-brown man, his tarry pigtail falling over the (4) s☐ou☐☐e☐ of his soiled blue coat, his hands ragged and scarred, with black, (5) ☐ro☐en nails, and the sabre cut across one cheek, a dirty, livid white. I remember him looking round the cover and (6) w☐i☐t☐ing to himself as he did so, and then breaking out in that old sea-song that he (7) s☐☐g so often afterwards:

> "Fifteen men on the dead man's chest–
> Yo-ho-ho, and a bottle of rum!"

in the high, old tottering (8) ☐o☐ce that seemed to have been tuned and broken at the capstan bars.

Then he (9) ☐a☐ped on the door with a bit of stick like a handspike that he carried, and when my father (10) ☐☐pe☐red, called roughly for a glass of rum. This, when it was brought to him, he drank slowly, like a connoisseur, lingering on the taste and still looking about him at the cliffs and up at our signboard.

Passage 11: An Extract from 'The War of the Worlds' by H.G. Wells

Letters have been removed from some of the words in this passage. Complete these words so that the passage makes sense.

No one would have believed in the last years of the nineteenth century that this world was being watched keenly and closely by intelligences greater than man's and yet as mortal as his own; that as men busied themselves about their various concerns they were scrutinised and (1) ☐tu☐☐ed, perhaps almost as narrowly as a man with a (2) ☐ic☐☐sco☐e might scrutinise the transient creatures that swarm and multiply in a drop of water. With (3) i☐fi☐it☐ complacency, men went to and fro over this (4) gl☐☐e about their little affairs, serene in their (5) ☐s☐☐ran☐e of their empire over matter. It is possible that the infusoria under the microscope do the same. No one gave a (6) ☐h☐ug☐t to the older worlds of space as sources of human danger, or thought of them only to dismiss the idea of life upon them as (7) i☐p☐☐si☐le or improbable.

It is curious to recall some of the mental habits of those departed days. At most, terrestrial men fancied there might be other men upon Mars, perhaps (8) ☐n☐er☐or to themselves and ready to welcome a missionary enterprise. Yet across the gulf of space, minds that are to our minds as ours are to those of the beasts that perish, intellects vast and cool and (9) ☐ns☐m☐ath☐t☐c, regarded this earth with (10) e☐v☐☐☐s eyes, and slowly and surely drew their plans against us. And early in the twentieth century came the great disillusionment.

Passage 12: The Helston Furry Dance

Letters have been removed from some of the words in this passage. Complete these words so that the passage makes sense.

Helston is a little town in Cornwall whose greatest claim to fame is the internationally (1) f☐☐ou☐ festival of the Furry (2) Da☐☐e. This is held every (3) y☐☐r on May 8th unless that day falls on a Sunday or Monday, when it is held on the (4) p☐☐ce☐i☐g Saturday.

Local legend states that (5) ☐en☐u☐i☐s ago, a fiery dragon dropped a stone on Helston. The (6) i☐h☐b☐☐an☐s at the time were so relieved that the town wasn't (7) d☐s☐☐o☐ed by the dragon that they (8) ce☐☐bra☐e☐ their deliverance by forming a line and dancing in and out of the houses, thus starting the (9) tr☐di☐☐☐n of the floral dance.

54

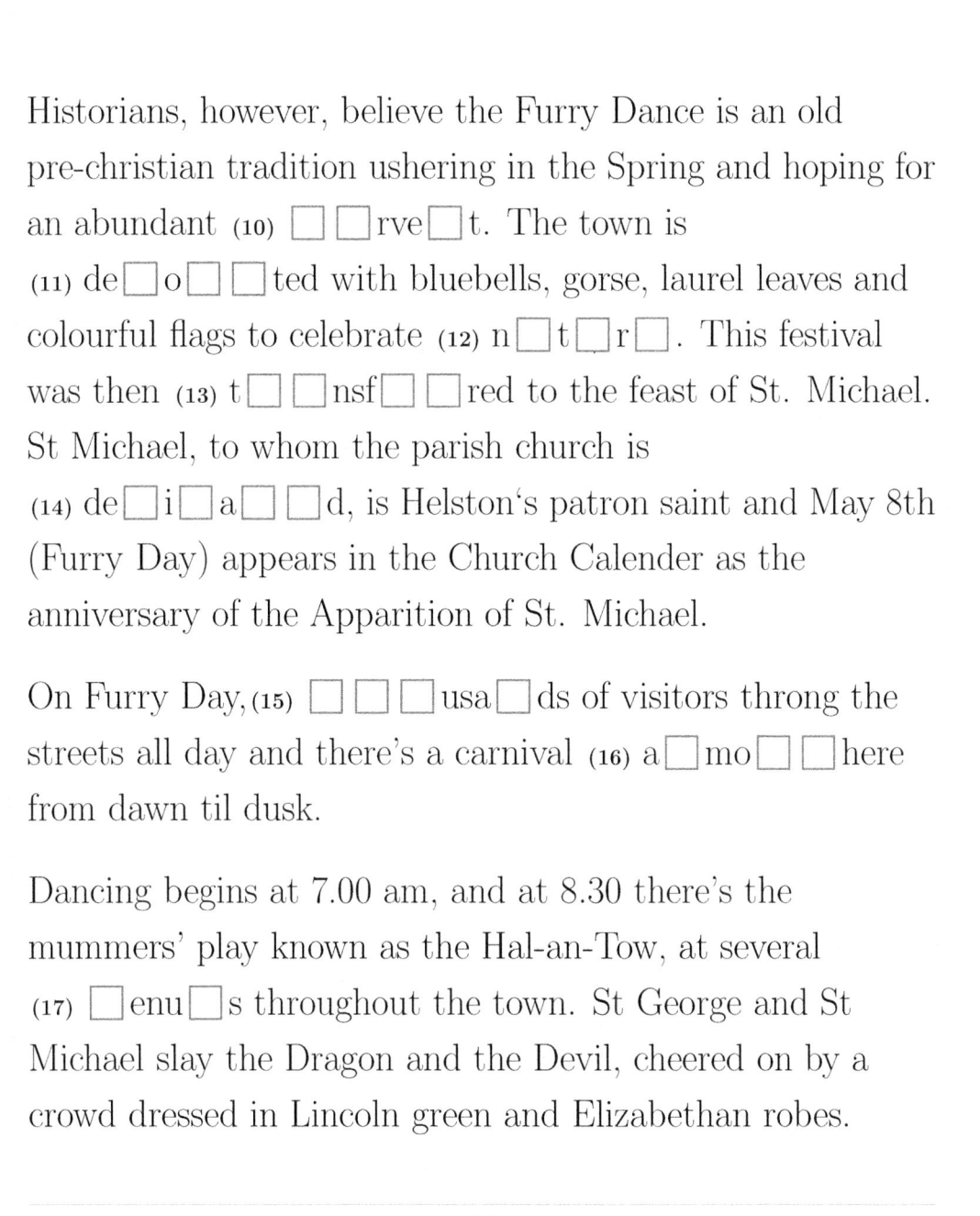

Historians, however, believe the Furry Dance is an old pre-christian tradition ushering in the Spring and hoping for an abundant (10) ☐☐rve☐t. The town is (11) de☐o☐☐ted with bluebells, gorse, laurel leaves and colourful flags to celebrate (12) n☐t☐r☐. This festival was then (13) t☐☐nsf☐☐red to the feast of St. Michael. St Michael, to whom the parish church is (14) de☐i☐a☐☐d, is Helston's patron saint and May 8th (Furry Day) appears in the Church Calender as the anniversary of the Apparition of St. Michael.

On Furry Day, (15) ☐☐☐usa☐ds of visitors throng the streets all day and there's a carnival (16) a☐mo☐☐here from dawn til dusk.

Dancing begins at 7.00 am, and at 8.30 there's the mummers' play known as the Hal-an-Tow, at several (17) ☐enu☐s throughout the town. St George and St Michael slay the Dragon and the Devil, cheered on by a crowd dressed in Lincoln green and Elizabethan robes.

The children of the town dance at 10.00 am, at midday there's the principal dance, with invited (18) p☐r☐☐ci☐☐nts in top hats, tails and dress gowns; and a final dance at 5.00 pm. The dancers weave in and out of the shops, houses and gardens behind the Helston Band playing the famous *Flora Dance*.

The Furry has been danced in Helston for centuries and is a day of great joy and fun but also a very elegant and colourful (19) ☐☐cas☐on.

Fill in the missing Letters Answers

Passage 1

1. landscapes
2. opportunities
3. especially
4. addition
5. formations
6. dinosaurs
7. tourists
8. originally
9. tranquil
10. watersports

Passage 2

1. mammals
2. oceans
3. species
4. world
5. climates
6. long
7. fish
8. young
9. summer
10. period
11. streamlined
12. speeds
13. environments
14. layer
15. insulate
16. survival

Passage 3

1. wealthy
2. career
3. travelled
4. broke
5. volunteered
6. appalled
7. conditions
8. transform
9. efficient
10. dramitically
11. comfortable
12. heroine
13. importance
14. recovery
15. contribution

Passage 4

1. flapping
2. beautifully
3. treetops
4. waddle
5. convenient
6. stump
7. elegantly
8. newspaper
9. Quack
10. sitting

Passage 5

1. dressed
2. assisted
3. except
4. bread
5. polished
6. operation
7. devoured
8. sucking
9. companions
10. starvation
11. hunger
12. afraid
13. believed
14. council
15. uniform
16. whispered
17. winked
18. desperate
19. advancing
20. more

Passage 6

1. nightly
2. rummage
3. articles
4. tidying
5. humourously
6. discoveries
7. understand
8. perplexing
9. appearence
10. admitted
11. childhood
12. stories

Passage 7

1. reigning
2. grandmother
3. monarch
4. celebrated
5. king
6. parents
7. broke
8. married
9. adopted
10. coronation

Passage 8

1. mountains
2. established
3. boasts
4. largest
5. picturesque
6. culture
7. population
8. summit
9. average
10. vanquished

Passage 9

1. Empire
2. conquered
3. invading
4. marched
5. except
6. Legend
7. stealthily
8. guarding
9. goddess
10. dwindling
11. loudly
12. courageous
13. launched
14. repelled
15. onwards
16. heroes

Passage 10

1. yesterday
2. plodding
3. behind
4. shoulder
5. broken
6. whistling
7. sang
8. voice
9. rapped
10. appeared

Passage 11

1. studied
2. microscope
3. infinite
4. globe
5. assurance
6. thought
7. impossible
8. inferior
9. unsympathetic
10. envious

Passage 12

1. famous
2. Dance
3. year
4. preceding
5. centuries
6. inhabitants
7. destroyed
8. celebrated
9. tradition
10. harvest
11. decorated
12. nature
13. transferred
14. dedicated
15. thousands
16. atmosphere
17. venues
18. participants
19. occasion

Passage 1: The Osprey

Choose the most appropriate word from the word bank to complete the following passage.

Word Bank						
world	spectacular	chore	anticipated	driving	ecosytems	
forlorn	garden	plot	species	fish	loaded	
fulfil	encounter	British	accommodation	book	

I was forty-four the first time I saw an osprey and it wasn't exactly the thrill I had (1) _____ . Like many children, as a youngster I was fascinated by wildlife. With the help of my Observer's (2) _____ of birds, I had managed to identify thirty-three species of birds visiting my parents' (3) _____ . This may not sound particularly (4) _____ to many people, but for a child growing up in Liverpool, I at least was impressed. There was, however one (5) _____ which really caught my imagination.

From the moment Blue Peter ran a story about a single pair of Ospreys breeding in Scotland, I longed to see one with my own eyes. Unfortunately, our family did not have a car and the ospreys may as well have been on the other side of the (6) _____ for all the chance I would have of seeing one. Maybe that was why, when my sons started pestering me to take them to Disney World, I began to hatch a (7) _____ .

I managed to persuade them that spending the whole holiday in theme parks would not give them a true feel of what Florida and its people were really like and that they really should visit one of the world's great (8) _____ – the Everglades.

To be fair, Orlando was more fun than I had thought it would be. But once the boys had well and truly had their fill of theme parks, it was time for me to finally (9) _____ the ambition I had held for thirty-five years. We (10) _____ up the car and headed south.

The nice thing about driving in America is that it is relatively easy. Sure, their aversion to roundabouts can make some of their city junctions a little confusing, but once you are out of town, driving is a real pleasure. We (11) _____ like to think that we are more law-abiding than most but, if you are doing fifty-seven down the freeway, you will find you are the fastest vehicle on the road. As a result, long-distance (12) _____ in the States is a very relaxed affair and the trip to the Everglades was more pleasure than (13) _____ . The other nice thing about road travel in America is how easy it is to find cheap (14) _____ . Roadside motels aren't exactly the Savoy, but most are clean and safe and it's easy to find one with a pool.

After a day and a half of travelling, I finally had my long dreamed-for (15) _____ with an osprey. We were driving along one of the incredibly long, straight roads in the park when the bird flew out of a drainage ditch carrying a large (16) _____ it had just caught. The bird came to within just four feet of me. That was the distance from the driver's seat to the passenger-side front wheel which flattened the bird into the tarmac. The last I saw of the bird was a (17) _____ little pile of feathers and fish scales drying in the sun.

Passage 2: Iceland

Choose the most appropriate word from the word bank to complete the following passage.

Word Bank				
settled	governed	forceful	transforms	located
dormant	population	renewable	unique	descendants
circle	major	steam	volcanoes	halfway

Iceland is an island (1) _____ midway between North America and mainland Europe. It lies just below the Arctic (2) _____ between 64 and 66 degrees north. Two-thirds of its (3) _____ of 300,000 live in its capital, Reykjavik. It is the northernmost capital in the world and is located exactly (4) _____ between New York and Moscow. It is the 18th largest island in the world and Europe's second largest island after Great Britain.

Iceland was (5) _____ by Vikings from Norway around 800 A.D. The native horses in the country today are direct (6) _____ from the horses the Vikings first brought over from mainland Europe. The country has been (7) _____ by the Althingi parliament since 930, and thus is the world's oldest existing parliamentary institution and makes Iceland the oldest democracy in the world. Viking settlement has given Iceland its (8) _____ cultural history.

However, the island is probably known most for its geological diversity: it has a wealth of volcanoes, geysers, glaciers and geothermic activity. Located on the Mid-Atlantic Ridge where the North American tectonic plate and the Eurasian plate meet, Iceland is divided in half by (9) _____ and is one of the most active volcanic areas in the world with a volcano erupting, on average, every four or five years. In the south of Iceland a volcano in Eyjafjallajökull erupted on March 21, 2010 for the first time since 1821. More eruptions in April were so (10) _____ and sent up huge clouds of ash that they caused (11) _____ disruption to air travel across Europe. There are still 30 to 40 active volcanoes on the island and hundreds more which are (12) _____ and haven't erupted for centuries.

Iceland has many geysers which are holes in the ground which spurt hot water. This geothermic activity is caused by surface water gradually seeping down through the ground until it meets rock heated by magma. The superheated water (13) _____ into steam, boiling violently throughout the channel in the ground so it rises quickly to the surface spurting boiling hot (14) _____ into the air. The English word geyser is derived from Iceland's most famous Geysir. Today Geysir doesn't erupt often, but nearby Strokkur erupts every eight to ten minutes. This geothermic energy under the ground has been harnessed by the Icelanders to produce cheap and (15) _____ energy. Iceland has a 99.96% renewable energy supply. The hot water is so cheap in Iceland that Icelanders are known for their long showers!

Passage 3: The Discovery

Choose the most appropriate word from the word bank to complete the following passage.

Word Bank				
allocated	concrete	equipment	aspect	degrees
sound	neighbours	jubilant	endear	privacy
main	stank	breakfast	acquired	fascinate

There was one (1) _____ of the new house which fascinated Peter. When they first moved in, he was dismayed to have been (2) _____ the smallest bedroom in the house. True, it was in a single-storey annexe at the side of the (3) _____ building which, as his parents pointed out, gave him more (4) _____ than if he had been in one of the larger bedrooms. However, it was rather small. The larger rooms were needed as bed and (5) _____ accommodation for paying guests, which was to be a useful income for his mum. The aspect of his tiny bedroom which did (6) _____ him however was the hollow sound which came when he walked across just one part of the floor near his bed. As soon as his parents had gone out for the evening to meet their new (7) _____ and he was assured of a bit of privacy, he set to removing the laminate flooring from that end of the room. Once he had done that, he was disappointed to discover that the floor appeared to consist of unbroken (8) _____ .

However, one spot still had a hollow (9) _____ to it when tapped. He was in the process of fetching a ten-pound sledge hammer from the shed when it occurred to him that bashing holes in his bedroom floor within days of moving in would not exactly (10) _____ him to his parents. Also, there was a good chance that what lay under his floor was just a sewage access point. In which case he would want to be able to seal it off again before he (11) _____ the house out.

Three days later, Peter had assembled the (12) _____ he would need to cut through the concrete and seal it again afterwards. He had found a long masonry drill in his father's shed and had bought a toughened steel saw with a narrow blade. To seal off the hole afterwards he had (13) _____ some silicone sealant and a strip of rubber just a little thicker than the saw blade. Finally, when he was ready, he waited until his parents went out again and then set about cutting through the floor. Using a school set-square as a guide, he drilled a circle of holes angling into the centre at thirty (14) _____ to the vertical. Sniffing near the first hole, he was relieved to discover that there was no smell of sewage and that gave him the confidence to carry on. There was a sudden lurch as the blades cut through into a cavity. Success! A (15) _____ Peter peered down into the space which had opened up in front of him. A set of stone steps descended down into a dark room....

Passage 4: Comets

Choose the most appropriate word from the word bank to complete the following passage.

Word Bank						
sparkle	vaporised	discovery	famous	concluded	asteroids
material	humans	approximately	celestial	mixture	orbit

Comets are small (1) _____ bodies which orbit the Sun. Unlike (2) _____ which are made up of rock, comets are mainly icy blocks made from frozen ammonia, methane and water and only contain a small amount of rock. Due to this, they are often nick-named 'dirty snowballs'. They have an elliptical (3) _____ just like the planets, however sometimes the ellipsis is quite extreme and as they travel close to the Sun, their ice melts and gases are emitted which (4) _____ in the light making them look like they have a firey tail.

Comets are made up of four components: the nucleus, coma, dust trail and ion trail. The nucleus is made up of rocky (5) _____ and can have a diameter of anything between 10 km and 100km. The Coma is the cloud of gases which are (6) _____ as the nucleus is heated as it approaches the sun. These gases are usually a (7) _____ of water vapour, ammonia, carbon dioxide. The trails are tiny dust particles blown away as the nucleus heats and ionised gases are blown away from the Sun.

Comets have been seen by (8) _____ for millions of years. However, scientists have (9) _____ that the lifespan of most comets it only thousands of years, which is relatively small compared to the age of our Solar System. There are (10) _____ 3000 known comets. There are several famous comets with Halley's Comet being possibly the most (11) _____ . In 1705, while studying the orbits of several known comets, Edmond Halley found that the comet observed in 1531, 1607 and 1682 was the same one. As a result of Halley's (12) _____ , the comet was named after him. Halley's Comet is visible every 75 to 76 years.

Passage 5: The Ghost

Choose the most appropriate word from the word bank to complete the following passage.

Word Bank				
thumb	skills	night	working	assistant
demonstration	hand	application	envelope	conclusion
stationery	evidence	unease	protocol	desk

Matilda Furnish picked up the envelope left on her (1) _____ . It was correctly addressed to her but there was no stamp - delivered by (2) _____ then. This was in itself a little puzzling. Anything delivered in the internal mail would have been stamped with the originating department. Also, Jane, her assistant should have taken the letter out of the (3) _____ before placing it in her in-tray. Finally, unless Her Majesty's Secret Services had gone all New-Age and arty while she wasn't watching, the choice of hand-made lilac (4) _____ was definitely unexpected. She pushed the inter-com button.

'Jane, who delivered the envelope on my desk?'

'I wasn't aware there was one. I haven't brought through your mail yet and no-one could have been in there since you left last (5) _____ .'

Furnish experienced a feeling of (6) _____ as she realised that she had, without thinking, opened the envelope while talking to her (7) _____ . This was against (8) _____ but, fortunately the contents didn't blow up in her face: what they proved to be was the most unusual job (9) _____ she had read for a while.

"Dear Ms Furnish,

Having given some thought to my (10) _____ and abilities, I have come to the (11) _____ that I am eminently suited to a position in your organisation. My ability to deliver this letter onto your desk is (12) _____ of my potential either as a burglar or an intelligence officer. Not having any desire, or need, to rob people of their belongings, I'm drawn to the conclusion that I should be (13) _____ for you. As a further (14) _____ of my ability to circumvent most security arrangements, you will find my (15) _____ -print on the fifth Post-It note down in your pad and also on the glass covering the photograph of the Queen on the wall behind your head.

Yours Sincerely, P."

Passage 6: Dinosaurs

Choose the most appropriate word from the word bank to complete the following passage.

Word Bank						
impact	crater	instantaneous	asteroid	accurately	tidal	
extinction	layer	demise	accepted	roamed	colliding	
scientific	palaeontologists	ecosystem	diameter	partially	vicinity	

The word Dinosaur translates as "terrible lizard" in the Greek Language. Dinosaurs are thought to have (1) _____ the Earth until about sixty-five million years ago when a mass planet (2) _____ event is thought to have occurred. Scientists and (3) _____ have put forward a variety of theories as to why the dinosaurs died out in such a short time. The most commonly (4) _____ theory is that a massive (5) _____ plunged to Earth kicking up enough dust and rubbish to block the Sun light from reaching the Earth's surface. This complete lack of sunlight resulted in a huge change to the planet's (6) _____ .

In 1980, Nobel Prize-winning physicist Luis Walter Alvarez and his geologist son Walter published a theory that an ancient (7) _____ of iridium-rich clay was caused by a large asteroid (8) _____ with Earth. There was (9) _____ devastation in the immediate (10) _____ and the widespread secondary effects of an asteroid (11) _____ caused the dinosaurs and many other animals to die out.

The impact site, known as the Chicxulub Crater, is centred on the Yucatán Peninsula in Mexico. It is now under the Ocean and although the meteor was approximately 10 – 15 kilometres wide, it hit the Earth with such speed and force that it left a (12) _____ approximately 150 kilometres in (13) _____ . The collision caused shock waves which in turn created (14) _____ waves and fires. The debris thrown into the air could have (15) _____ blocked out the sun which would have had an effect on plant-life. Weather patterns changed and as plants died, the animals further up the food chain also died.

The mystery of the sudden extinction of the dinosaurs can be dated fairly (16) _____ with modern (17) _____ methods. The clay that started this theory, can now be dated to within two thousand years which matched in exactly with the (18) _____ of the dinosaurs.

Passage 7: Extract from 'A Journey to the centre of the Earth' by Jules Verne

Choose the most appropriate word from the word bank to complete the following passage.

Word Bank				
ambitious	excellent	staircase	payment	despair
translucent	shivering	drunken	appeared	crawling
ascended	possible	upwards	optical	followed

It was impossible to dispute the dictatorial commands of my uncle. I yielded with a groan. On (1) _____ of a fee, a verger gave us the key. He, for one, was not partial to the ascent. My uncle at once showed me the way, running up the steps like a schoolboy. I (2) _____ as well as I could, though no sooner was I outside the tower, than my head began to swim. There was nothing of the eagle about me. The earth was enough for me, and no (3) _____ desire to soar ever entered my mind. Still things did not go badly until I had (4) _____ 150 steps, and was near the platform, when I began to feel the rush of cold air. I could scarcely stand, when clutching the railings, I looked (5) _____. The railing was frail enough, but nothing to those which skirted the terrible winding (6) _____, that appeared, from where I stood, to ascend to the skies. "Now then, Henry."

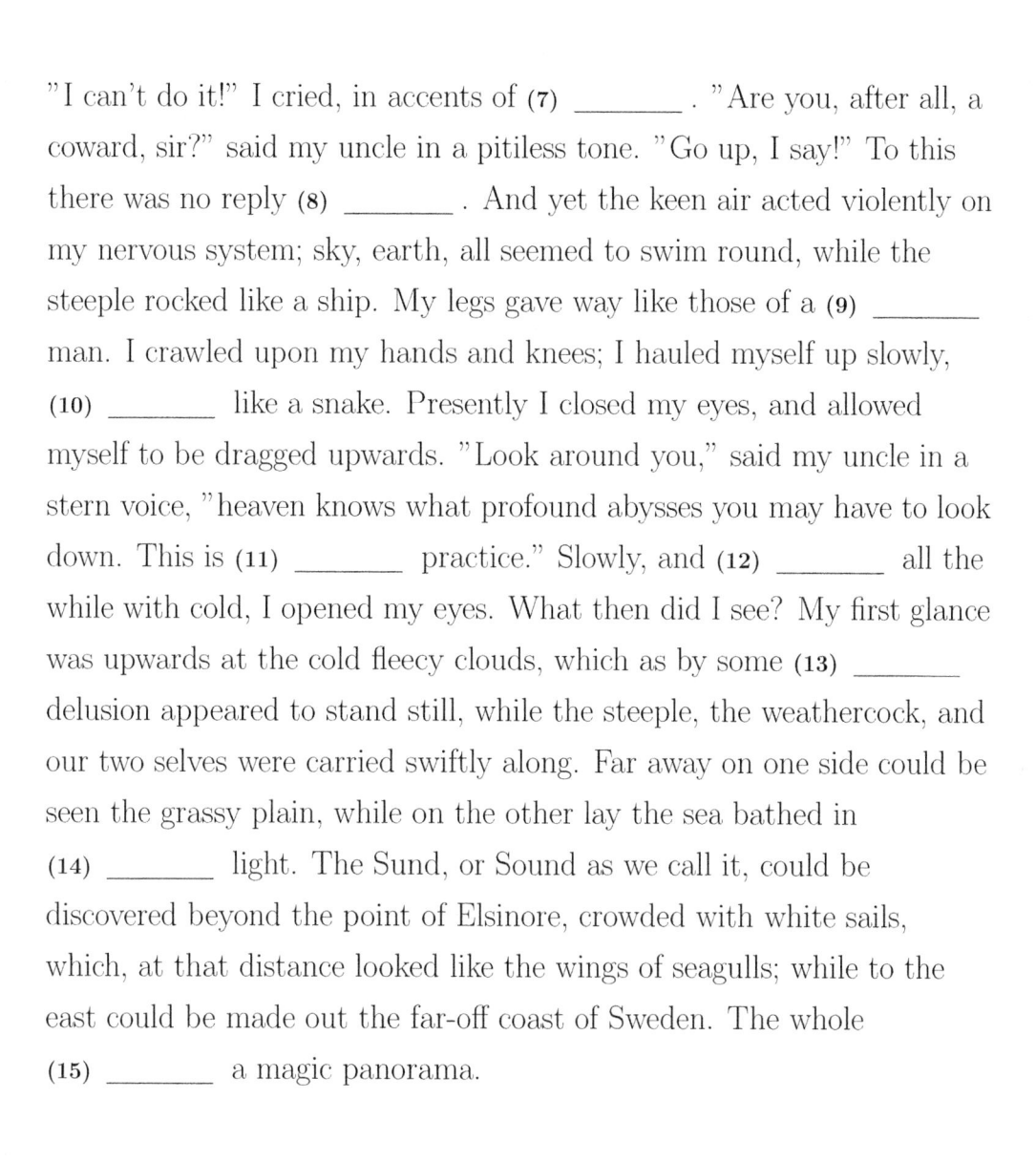

"I can't do it!" I cried, in accents of (7) _____. "Are you, after all, a coward, sir?" said my uncle in a pitiless tone. "Go up, I say!" To this there was no reply (8) _____. And yet the keen air acted violently on my nervous system; sky, earth, all seemed to swim round, while the steeple rocked like a ship. My legs gave way like those of a (9) _____ man. I crawled upon my hands and knees; I hauled myself up slowly, (10) _____ like a snake. Presently I closed my eyes, and allowed myself to be dragged upwards. "Look around you," said my uncle in a stern voice, "heaven knows what profound abysses you may have to look down. This is (11) _____ practice." Slowly, and (12) _____ all the while with cold, I opened my eyes. What then did I see? My first glance was upwards at the cold fleecy clouds, which as by some (13) _____ delusion appeared to stand still, while the steeple, the weathercock, and our two selves were carried swiftly along. Far away on one side could be seen the grassy plain, while on the other lay the sea bathed in (14) _____ light. The Sund, or Sound as we call it, could be discovered beyond the point of Elsinore, crowded with white sails, which, at that distance looked like the wings of seagulls; while to the east could be made out the far-off coast of Sweden. The whole (15) _____ a magic panorama.

Passage 8: The Discovery of Penicillin

Choose the most appropriate word from the word bank to complete the following passage.

Word Bank					
Hospitals	introduction	advances	granted	manufactured	insignificant
bacteria	benefits	States	casualties	types	invasion
governments	treatment	produce	cure		

The discovery of penicillin in the 1940s has been classed as one of the greatest (1) _____ in medicine. It was discovered by Alexander Fleming, in 1928. He was a professor of Bacteriology in London and had left some petri dishes containing bacteria which cause boils and sore throats by a window before he went on holiday. When he came back, he noticed that mould had grown in parts of the dishes. In those parts, the (2) _____ had been killed. He realised that this mould, later identified as a rare strain of *Penicillium notatum*, killed other (3) _____ of bacteria too.

Before its (4) _____ , there was no effective (5) _____ for infections such as pneumonia, infected injuries etc. (6) _____ were full of people with blood poisoning contracted from a cut or a scratch, and doctors could do little to (7) _____ them but wait and hope that they would get better. However, it took years of research to create an antibiotic which could be given to humans and also (8) _____ on an industrial scale.

It was Howard Florey who took his penicillin over to the United (9) _____ in 1941 and persuaded the bigger and wealthier pharmaceutical companies to (10) _____ penicillin on a larger industrial scale. World War II made production difficult but equally, the (11) _____ of large supplies of antibiotics was obvious to the (12) _____ of both UK and USA. One of the major goals was to have an adequate supply of the drug on hand for the proposed D-Day (13) _____ of Europe where it was expected that there would be large numbers of (14) _____ needing this medicine.

Antibiotics are compounds produced by bacteria and fungi which are capable of killing, or inhibiting, competing microbial species. There are actually just 7 strains of antibiotics, but various mutations of these strains have been made. We take antibiotics for (15) _____ in our treatment of illnesses and injuries, but if it hadn't been for that chance discovery by Fleming, people might still be dying from illnesses which we think are (16) _____ today.

Passage 9: The invention of the modern flushing toilet

Choose the most appropriate word from the word bank to complete the following passage.

Word Bank				
unhygienic	described	located	techniques	bucket
Elizabethan	prototype	running	home	civilisations
required	Primitive	Palace	delivered	descend

Today, we take it for granted that we have (1) _____ water and a flushable toilet in our bathrooms but this has not always been the case. (2) _____ toilets (often called latrines) date back thousands of years and early toilet systems which used running water from streams used by various ancient (3) _____ such as the Romans. However, the flush toilet has its origins in (4) _____ England.

Sir John Harington first (5) _____ an idea for a flushable toilet in 1596. Sir John was a courtier and godson of Queen Elizabeth I. He devised a toilet which used an oval bowl which had been water-proofed by covering it in type of tar called pitch. Water was (6) _____ to the toilet from a tank which held the water called a cistern. This was (7) _____ on a floor higher up than the toilet so that the water could (8) _____ easily. The only drawback to this design was that it (9) _____ 7.5 gallons of water for each flush!

However, Sir John suggested that 20 people could use the toilet between each flush. This seems ridiculous and (10) _____ to us nowadays, but at the time, it was an immense improvement on the hole in the floor or simple (11) _____ which had gone before.

Although Harington installed a working (12) _____ of his toilet for Queen Elizabeth at Richmond (13) _____ , it would take centuries and huge improvements in both manufacturing (14) _____ and waste disposal before the flush toilet would appear in every (15) _____ .

Passage 10: An extract from 'Tom Sawyer' by Mark Twain

Choose the most appropriate word from the word bank to complete the following passage.

Word Bank					
resumed	attention	sorrows	dreading	nibbling	apple
reluctance	melancholy	operation	wealth	discouraged	consent
inspiration	move	uttered	rat	contemplated	bucket
light	tackle	magnificent	watered		

Tom appeared on the sidewalk with a (1) _____ of whitewash paint and a long-handled brush. He surveyed the fence and a deep (2) _____ settled down upon his spirit. Thirty yards of board fence nine feet high. Sighing, he dipped his brush and passed it along the topmost plank; repeated the (3) _____ ; did it again; compared the insignificant whitewashed streak with the far-reaching continent of unwhitewashed fence, and sat down on a tree-box (4) _____ .

He began to think of the fun he had planned for this day, and his (5) _____ multiplied. At this dark and hopeless moment an (6) _____ burst upon him! Nothing less than a great, (7) _____ inspiration.

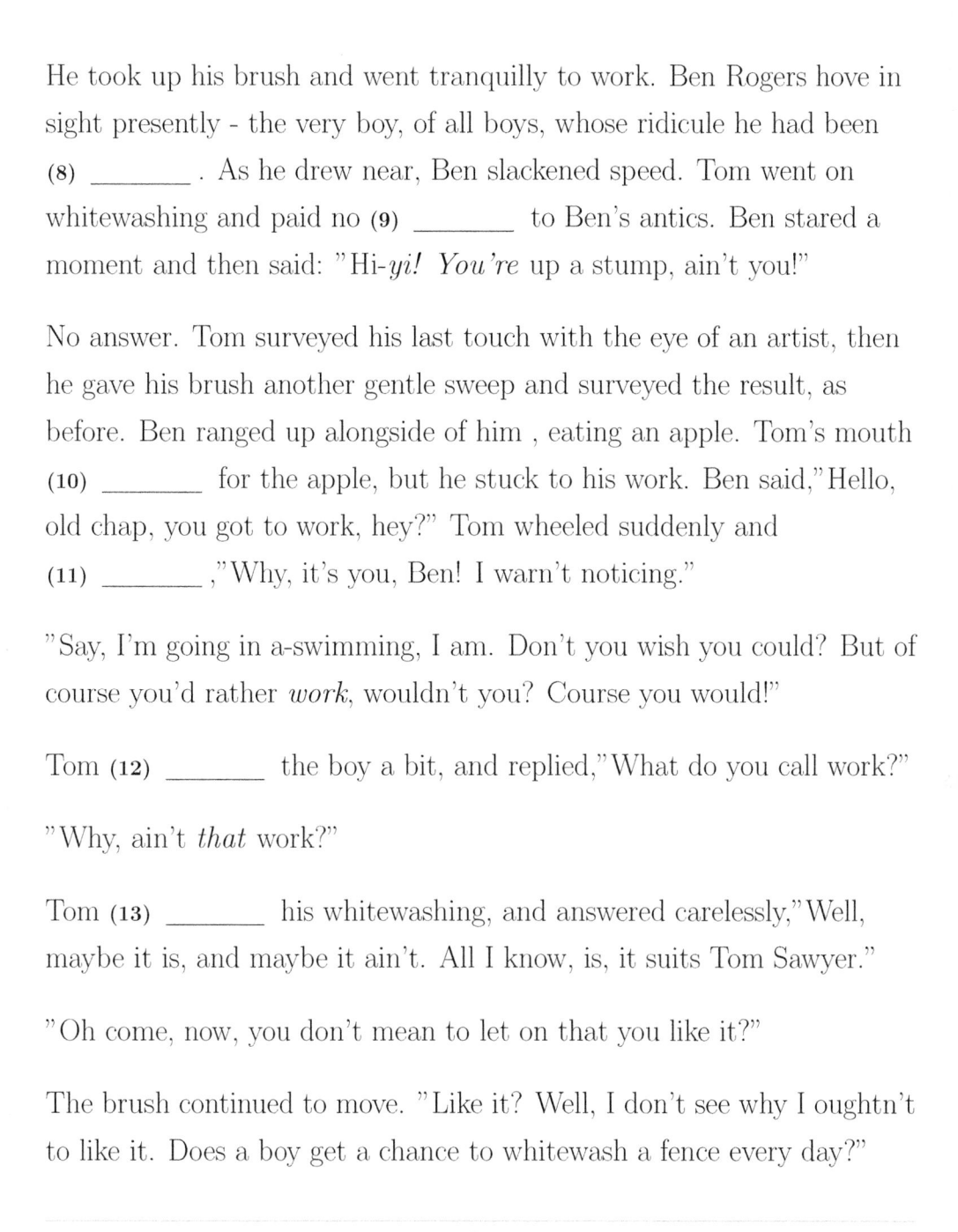

He took up his brush and went tranquilly to work. Ben Rogers hove in sight presently - the very boy, of all boys, whose ridicule he had been (8) _____ . As he drew near, Ben slackened speed. Tom went on whitewashing and paid no (9) _____ to Ben's antics. Ben stared a moment and then said: "Hi-*yi! You're* up a stump, ain't you!"

No answer. Tom surveyed his last touch with the eye of an artist, then he gave his brush another gentle sweep and surveyed the result, as before. Ben ranged up alongside of him , eating an apple. Tom's mouth (10) _____ for the apple, but he stuck to his work. Ben said,"Hello, old chap, you got to work, hey?" Tom wheeled suddenly and (11) _____ ,"Why, it's you, Ben! I warn't noticing."

"Say, I'm going in a-swimming, I am. Don't you wish you could? But of course you'd rather *work*, wouldn't you? Course you would!"

Tom (12) _____ the boy a bit, and replied,"What do you call work?"

"Why, ain't *that* work?"

Tom (13) _____ his whitewashing, and answered carelessly,"Well, maybe it is, and maybe it ain't. All I know, is, it suits Tom Sawyer."

"Oh come, now, you don't mean to let on that you like it?"

The brush continued to move. "Like it? Well, I don't see why I oughtn't to like it. Does a boy get a chance to whitewash a fence every day?"

That put the thing in a new (14) _____ . Ben stopped (15) _____ his apple. Tom swept his brush daintily back and forth, stepped back to note the effect, added a touch here and there , criticised the effect again. Ben watched every (16) _____ and getting more and more interested, more and more absorbed. Presently, he said, "Say, Tom, let *me* whitewash a little."

Tom considered, was about to (17) _____ ; but he altered his mind:"No. No - I reckon it wouldn't hardly do, Ben. You see, Aunt Polly's awful particular about this fence - right here on the street, you know - but if it was the back fence I wouldn't mind and *she* wouldn't. Yes, she's awful particular about this fence; it's got to be done very careful; I reckon there ain't one boy in a thousand, maybe two thousand, that can do it the way it's got to be done."

"No - is that so? Oh come now, lemme just try. Only just a little - I'd let *you*, if you was me, Tom."

"Ben, I'd like to, honest; but Aunt Polly - well, Jim wanted to do it, but she wouldn't let him; Sid wanted to do it, and she wouldn't let Sid. Now don't you see how I'm fixed? If you was to (18) _____ this fence and anything was to happen to it..."

"Oh, shucks, I'll be just as careful. Now lemme try. Say, I'll give you the core of my apple."

"Well, here - No, Ben, now don't. I'm afeard..."

"I'll give you *all* of it!"

Tom gave up the brush with (19) _____ in his face, but alacrity in his heart. And while the late steamer Big Missouri worked and sweated in the sun, the retired artist sat on a barrel in the shade close by, dangled his legs, munched his (20) _____ , and planned the slaughter of more innocents. There was no lack of material; boys happened along every little while; they came to jeer, but remained to whitewash. By the time Ben was tired out, Tom had traded the next chance to Billy Fisher for a kite, in good repair; and when he played out, Johnny Miller bought in for a dead (21) _____ and a string to swing it with - and so on, and so on, hour after hour. And when the middle of the afternoon came, from being a poor poverty-stricken boy in the morning, Tom was literally rolling in (22) _____ . He had besides the things before mentioned, twelve marbles, part of a jews-harp, a piece of blue bottle-glass to look through, a spool cannon, a key that wouldn't unlock anything, a fragment of chalk, a glass stopper of a decanter, a tin soldier, a couple of tadpoles, six fire-crackers, a kitten with only one eye, a brass doorknob, a dog-collar - but no dog - the handle of a knife, four pieces of orange-peel, and a dilapidated old window sash.

He had had a nice, good, idle time all the while - plenty of company - and the fence had three coats of whitewash on it! If he hadn't run out of whitewash he would have bankrupted every boy in the village.

Word Bank Answers

Passage 1

1. anticipated
2. book
3. garden
4. spectacular
5. species
6. world
7. plot
8. ecosystems
9. fulfil
10. loaded
11. British
12. driving
13. chore
14. accommodation
15. encounter
16. fish
17. forlorn

Passage 2

1. located
2. Circle
3. population
4. halfway
5. settled
6. descendants
7. governed
8. unique
9. volcanoes
10. forceful
11. major
12. dormant
13. transforms
14. steam
15. renewable

Passage 3

1. aspect
2. allocated
3. main
4. privacy
5. breakfast
6. fascinate
7. neighbours
8. concrete
9. sound
10. endear
11. stank
12. equipment
13. acquired
14. degrees
15. jubilant

Passage 4

1. celestial
2. asteroids
3. orbit
4. sparkle
5. material
6. vaporised
7. mixture
8. humans
9. concluded
10. approximately
11. famous
12. discovery

Passage 5

1. desk
2. hand
3. envelope
4. stationery
5. night
6. unease
7. assistant
8. protocol
9. application
10. skills
11. conclusion
12. evidence
13. working
14. demonstration
15. thumb

Passage 6

1. roamed
2. extinction
3. palaeontologists
4. accepted
5. asteroid
6. ecosystem
7. layer
8. colliding
9. instantaneous
10. vicinity
11. impact
12. crater
13. diameter
14. tidal
15. partially
16. accurately
17. scientific
18. demise

Passage 7

1. payment
2. followed
3. ambitious
4. ascended
5. upwards
6. staircase
7. despair
8. possible
9. drunken
10. crawling
11. excellent
12. shivering
13. optical
14. translucent
15. appeared

Passage 8

1. advances
2. bacteria
3. types
4. introduction
5. treatment
6. Hospitals
7. cure
8. manufactured
9. States
10. produce
11. benefits
12. governments
13. invasion
14. casualties
15. granted
16. insignificant

Passage 9

1. running
2. Primitive
3. civilisations
4. Elizabethan
5. described
6. delivered
7. located
8. descend
9. required
10. unhygienic
11. bucket
12. prototype
13. Palace
14. techniques
15. home

Passage 10

1. bucket
2. melancholy
3. operation
4. discouraged
5. sorrows
6. inspiration
7. magnificent
8. dreading
9. attention
10. surveyed
11. uttered
12. contemplated
13. resumed
14. light
15. nibbling
16. move
17. consent
18. tackle
19. reluctance
20. apple
21. rat
22. wealth